THE
MIGHTY WARRIORS

GEORGE SMITH

PATTON, JR.
THE
LOST ROMANTIC

by
ALLAN CARPENTER

Rourke Publications Inc.
Vero Beach, Florida 32964

EDITORIAL ACKNOWLEDGMENTS
Illustrations
WESLEY KLUG
Assistant to the Author
and Indexer
CARL PROVORSE
Typography by
LAW BULLETIN PUBLISHING COMPANY

Published by Rourke Publications, Inc.
Vero Beach, FL 32964
© 1987 Rourke Publications Inc. All rights reserved. No part of this book may be reproduced or utilized in any form or by any means, electronic or mechanical including photocopying, recording or by any information storage and retrieval system, without permission in writing from the publisher.

Library of Congress Cataloging-in-Publication Data
Carpenter, Allan, 1917-
George Smith Patton: The Lost Romantic.
(The Mighty Warriors)
Bibliography: p.
Includes index.
Summary: Traces the life and career of the outspoken
general who served in World Wars I and II. Includes
some of his writings.
1. Patton, George S. (George Smith), 1885-1945—
Juvenile literature. 2. Generals—United States—
Biography—Juvenile literature. 3. United States.
Army—Biography—Juvenile literature. 4. United
States— History, Military—20th century—Juvenile
literature. [1. Patton, George S. (George Smith),
1885-1945, 2. Generals I.] Title. II Series.
E745.P3C37 1987 355'.0092'4 [B] [92] 87-9841
ISBN 0-86625-329-7

Cover portrait, formal army portrait; illustration by Wesley Klug; previous pages, Patton memorabilia at Patton Museum, includes his famous "pearl-handled" revolvers.

CONTENTS

Chapter One
The Mechanized Mexican 7

Chapter Two
A Heritage Of Wealth And War 12

Chapter Three
Back To The Revolution 15

Chapter Four
Maternal Distinctions 19

Chapter Five
A Pampered Aristocrat. 22

Chapter Six
Not Much Of A Scholar 26

Chapter Seven
A Real Helpmate. 30

Chapter Eight
Saber George 33

Chapter Nine
Military Olympics. 35

Chapter Ten
On To Mexico 40

Chapter Eleven
The Prehistoric Penny 45

Chapter Twelve
Tanks At Last 47

Chapter Thirteen
Tank Religion—A New Doctrine 52

Chapter Fourteen
Waiting For Another War 56

Chapter Fifteen
The Warhorse Stirs 62

Chapter Sixteen
Carrying The "Torch" 64

Chapter Seventeen
"The Slap Heard 'Round The World" 68

Chapter Eighteen
Eisenhower's Reprimand 74

Chapter Nineteen
"Kick Him While He's Down" 78

Chapter Twenty
The Speedy Third 81

Chapter Twenty-One
Politics! Politics! Politics! 88

Chapter Twenty-Two
Complex and Controversial 94

APPENDIX

Highlights 98
Some Sources Of Further Information 100
What He Said 101
Index 108
Acknowledgments 112

Chapter One

THE MECHANIZED MEXICAN

The cloud of dust appeared on the horizon; as it came closer, those waiting for it could make out an automobile approaching across the gloomy desert landscape, bringing a good portion of the dusty ground with it. The first car was accompanied by other cars and cavalry troops.

As the lead car grew closer, the waiting crowd could see a strange object strapped to the hood; it looked like—could it be?

The driver of the car was a young American cavalry officer named George Smith Patton, Jr. He was just bringing to a close a strange episode in which he had pioneered two firsts in American history.

The dusty landscape was the semi-desert wasteland of northern Mexico not too far from the

Following page, the young officer in Mexico already showed traces of his genius. In this rare portrait he is shown smoking his famous pipe and surveying the Mexican scene, perhaps trying to spot Pancho Villa.

U.S. border. The presence of U.S. troops in Mexican territory had raised worldwide fears of a North American war.

Several groups of Mexican leaders had been fighting among themselves to control the government of Mexico. Mexican leader Francisco "Pancho" Villa had lost out in his bid to govern the country. He fled to northern Mexico where he fought the troops of the recognized government as a guerrilla leader.

In 1915 American President Woodrow Wilson had recognized Villa's foe, Venustiano Carranza, as the rightful leader of Mexico.

This action enraged Villa. Some of his men captured a group of American men who were mining in Mexico and shot them in cold blood. Then another group of Mexicans who were thought to be a part of Villa's forces swept across the U.S. border into the New Mexican town of Columbus. Several U.S. citizens were killed before the guerrillas were driven back into Mexico.

Villa said he was not responsible for these actions, but easygoing President Wilson was finally driven into action. He ordered famed General John J. Pershing to invade Mexico, capture Villa and put an end to such offenses against the U.S.

On March 13, 1916, Pershing crossed the border on his mission against Villa. With him as an aide was young Lieutenant George Patton, eager as he always had been to get into a real fight at last.

Northern Mexico is a wind-swept and desolate country. Pershing's scouting parties rode across the semi desert reaches trying to run down the elusive guerrillas. The horse soldiers were accompanied by some early autos and trucks.

It was George Patton's good luck to run into a group of Villa's outlaws led by renegade General Julio Cardenas.

The two forces engaged in a fire fight. Young George received his baptism of fire and loved it. When it was over, Patton had killed General Cardenas and both his assistants.

In earlier times the bodies of the slain leader and his aides might have been strapped to the backs of horses and brought back to show the success of the victors. Patton thought up a strange new twist. He strapped the general's body to the hood of one of the old Dodge cars and started back to the American camp.

This exotic procession was greeted with surprised cheers and hurrahs, as the first real success of what has been called the Punitive Expedition into Mexico. The American forces were never successful in rounding up Villa, and World War I soon forced them to turn to more important matters.

Nevertheless, Patton's success has gone into the record books as the first use of "mechanized" forces in modern warfare. The day of the American automobile and its armored successors had arrived as a part of the armed services.

The young American officer who first used the Dodge, the Model T and other cars as a part of a fighting force was to become the world's greatest expert in mechanized warfare.

Chapter Two

A HERITAGE OF WEALTH AND WAR

The family background and early life of George Smith Patton, Jr. had much to do with his success as a military leader. His upbringing may also have contributed to some of his attitudes and actions which later reflected unfavorably on his character.

Although the modern general was known as "junior," he actually was the third to bear that name. His early years were full of tales told of the thrilling and terrible times endured by his ancestors in the Civil War. His father, though too young to fight, had stored up clear recollections of the war, of the Confederacy and of his acquaintances who had some part in the war.

The first George Smith Patton was only twenty-six when he was killed at the Battle of

Winchester in the Shenandoah Valley, which had been defended so brilliantly by General Stonewall Jackson. This first wartime Patton was commanding the twenty-second Virginia Regiment at the time he was killed.

The first Patton's brother, also lost his life during the Civil War. He was leading a regiment commanded by Major General George E. Pickett during that latter's famous charge in the Battle of Gettysburg.

Altogether, six of those brothers, sons of John Mercer Patton, took part in the Civil War. Two other sons stayed at home because they were not old enough to fight.

As the modern general was growing up, his home was filled with mementos and conversations about the Civil War, about how it was carried out, about its successes and failures and the sacrifices of those who served and of those who stayed at home.

In honored places in the home were steel engravings of General Robert E. Lee and General Stonewall Jackson. Ruth Ellen Patten Totten, daughter of the World War II Patton, said that "Until he was fifteen years old, my father thought those steel engravings were of God and Jesus Christ." If not an exaggeration, her statement is a rather unfortunate commentary on the young man's perception.

Another and rather gruesome memento of the Civil War was the shell fragment taken from the body of the first George Patton and also carefully preserved in young George's home.

George's father had many Civil War friends who filled the young man with tales and reminiscences of war. This kind of talk did much to instill Patton's later glorification of war and the stimulation of battle.

One of the most famous of those friends often visited the family and recalled his favorite wartime stories. This was Colonel John Mosby, who was known as the "Grey Ghost" of J.E.B. Stuart's dashing cavalry. The aging colonel would help the young George to reenact some of his war experiences. While he played himself, George would take the part of General Robert E. Lee, and the young and the old pretended to dash around on their horses.

Chapter Three

BACK TO THE REVOLUTION

Some members of the aristocratic Patton family claimed to trace their ancestry back to some of the signers of the Magna Charta, that great first document on which British and American freedoms were later built. Another branch of the family has legitimate claims of relationship to George Washington, through a Patton uncle, John Washington.

In any event, on his father's side the future World War II general had interesting connections with European ancestors and with the Revolutionary War. For some reason now forgotten to history, during the eighteenth century a young man from Aberdeen, Scotland, had been forced to leave his native country and flee to America, making his way finally to Fredericksburg, Virginia.

The real name of the young man is not known today. He probably had good reasons for hiding it in his new homeland, where he called himself Robert Patton. With a new name, a new home and a new beginning, Patton became safe from any authorities who might have wanted to track him down.

A person of apparent ability, Robert Patton made a fortune and married successfully. His wife was Anna Gordon Mercer. As the only daughter of Dr. Hugh Mercer, she lent distinction to the family tree. Her physician father served under George Washington in General Braddock's push against Fort Duquesne in 1756. The doctor became Surgeon-General of the American forces in the Revolutionary War.

A son of Robert Patton and Anna Mercer Patton, John Mercer Patton, was the father of the first George Smith Patton, the grandfather of the modern day General Patton.

After the first George Smith Patton was buried as a Civil War Confederate Brigadier General, his widow remarried a Colonel George H. Smith. With her two sons and a daughter, she and her new husband left for California, not long after the end of the Civil War.

Previous pages, the family portrait of 1900 shows the future general at fifteen (left), his mother, Ruth Wilson Patton, father, George S. Patton and sister, Anne Wilson Patton, at Lake Vineyard, San Gabriel, California.

Chapter Four

MATERNAL DISTINCTIONS

The third generation George Smith Patton, of World War II fame, came from an even more distinguished background on his mother's side.

Her family history in America begins with fifteen-year-old Benjamin Davis Wilson. At that age Wilson was already operating a trading post near present Vicksburg, Mississippi, doing a flourishing business with the Choctaw Indians of the area.

As the American West opened, Wilson became a trapper for the Rocky Mountain Fur Company. Trapping in New Mexico, he was captured by the Apache Indians but managed to get away from his captors. Later, in California, Wilson was hit by a poisoned Indian arrow, but again survived and decided to seek his fortune in China.

Wilson waited at the port of a tiny California town, but when no China-bound ship appeared, he decided to stay where he was. No one knew, of course, that the tiny village called El Pueblo de Nuestra Senora la Reina de Los Angeles de Porciuncula would some day become America's second largest city, known simply as Los Angeles.

Benjamin Wilson not only grew with the town but also became one of its wealthiest and most famous citizens, a member of the local aristocracy, given the Spanish title Don during the time of Mexican control. In the frontier days of conflict with the local Indians and bandits, Wilson was known as a feared and fearsome fighter. After one raid against hostile Indians, Wilson was said to have returned with "basket-loads" of Indian heads.

Despite his seeming lack of mercy, Wilson was one of the first to call for justice to the displaced Indians. As American Indian agent, he came to feel strongly that the Indian was the one who needed protection, not the other way around.

This extraordinary man introduced the practice of growing grapes for wine in California. He planted the first citrus in the region and experimented with growing cane for sugar. While California was still under Mexican control, he was known as Don Benito, and he was the Alcalde, or leader, of La Pueblo de Nuestra Senora la Reina de Los Angeles de Parciuncula and became mayor of the city when it became American Los Angeles. He also saw service as a state senator for three terms.

After his first wife died, Wilson married Margaret S. Hereford of Los Angeles. Their daughter, Ruth Smith Wilson, married the George Patton who was the son of the Civil War commander. George and Ruth Patton were the parents of the George Smith Patton who was destined to become the most controversial of all the controversial figures of World War II.

George Smith Patton, jr., at age seven.

Chapter Five

A PAMPERED ARISTOCRAT

What a family background for a young man—the heir of family fortunes and a heritage of war and wealth stretching from one coast of America to the other!

It is, perhaps, easy to surmise where the World War II Patton inherited the "blood and guts" for which he was famous. He was a grandson of the Civil War, of the Indian wars and came from pioneer California stock. Perhaps the latter was the most important in the modern commander's fierce resolve.

His grandfather, Benjamin Wilson, it was told, would dare almost anything. On one occasion he loaned young Colonel Claus Spreckles $5,000 on a simple handshake. When Wilson demanded the return of the money after Spreckles was well on his way to becoming the great sugar baron of

America, he was told that since there was no official record of the loan it would not be paid back.

Wilson, it was said, buckled on his gunbelt, entered Spreckles' office and said to the male secretary, "Young man, you have never seen death? Well, then, wait about one minute." Apparently the secretary hurried in to tell his boss that he was about to be shot. In any event, the loan was quickly repaid.

Into such an extraordinary heritage young George Smith Patton, Jr., was born on November 11, 1885, a day on which 33 years later he would celebrate the end of a great world war. Young Patton spent his early years on the great ranch inherited by his father.

No one is quite certain why the parents kept him from a formal education until he was eleven years old. There is some speculation that George suffered from dyslexia. This is a disorder that affects the connection between the brain and the eyes, which makes it difficult to read and write. Modern specialists recognize this condition and know how to help those afflicted with it, but not much was known about it while George was growing up.

If he did have to overcome this problem, he made a remarkable success of it. In later years he became a writer and speaker of extraordinary ability. Over the years he gathered one of the largest personal libraries of military materials, and most of these were covered with notes in his own hand. He added seven typewritten pages of observation about one of his favorites.

It may be that it was not dyslexia that kept him out of school. More likely, his father's theory of education may have been responsible for his unique educational background. The senior Patton was convinced that children could learn best by being read to by the older people around them. The father argued that children learned more quickly by ear than by eye, and that listening to the sound of great literature was more meaningful for young people than reading by themselves.

George enjoyed and benefited from this process in some ways, but was apparently deprived in others. By the time he was seven years old he could quote entire pages from Homer's *Iliad* as translated by Pope.

Opposite, looking like a mature young man in the "dress-up" costume of the day, Patton at age ten.

Chapter Six

NOT MUCH OF A SCHOLAR

However, when he entered Stephen Cutter Clark's Classical School for Boys at Pasadena, George Smith Patton, Jr., could neither read nor write. He understood the world of ideas and could quote from the ideas of most of the learned writers, but he could not produce a theme of his own or work simple arithmetic.

He must have made substantial progress in elementary education before he entered Pasadena High School, because he managed to graduate from that institution. In preparation for a hoped-for career at West Point, young George spent the school year of 1903-04 at Virginia Military Institute, where his father had been a graduate.

With his background of military forebears

and family wealth and influence, it is not surprising that George was admitted to the military academy at West Point in 1904 despite his shortcomings in mathematics.

At the end of his first year he had failed in French. To continue his studies, he was required to pass a test in French and for some strange reason also one in mathematics, which he had somehow managed to pass. Perversely, he managed to pass the French test but failed in mathematics. However, he was permitted to return to the academy for another round as a first-year Plebe, so that he required five years to graduate instead of four. His unusual record of almost no demerits was one of the factors in his being readmitted.

Patton was devoted to football and played it with such abandon that he broke both of his arms in the game. He did go on, however, to win the Army letter which he fought so hard for by starring in track, breaking the record in the 220-yard low hurdles.

Always certain of his own abilities, Patton was said to be too "cocksure of himself" to be very popular with his classmates during student years, but he was generally admired by them for his real abilities. One account called him "...a bad student but a good sailor, winning several sailing championships."

In spite of some mild failings George Smith Patton graduated from West Point on June ll,

1909. At the time, he was class adjutant, one of the two highest undergraduate honors. Commissioned as a second lieutenant of cavalry, Patton looked forward to a successful career, fired with fierce ambition.

Opposite, the high ranking graduate of West Point shows in his graduation picture the courage and determination which were to carry George S. Patton, Jr., through a lifetime of service to his country.

Chapter Seven

A REAL HELPMATE

While George was younger, the Patton family often vacationed on the Island of Catalina, off the California coast. It was a fashionable place, especially in the summer when society often gathered there. In those summers the Pattons saw a good deal of the Frederick Ayers. The families were distantly related through George's aunt, Ophelia Smith.

Most summers the Ayers had their children with them, Katherine, Frederick, Jr., and Beatrice. Beatrice and George were often thrown together, and she found him appealing. He was then a tall slender youth of fourteen and she thirteen. It was then, apparently, that Beatrice decided to marry George. As they continued to meet in summer on the island, Beatrice became an attractive young lady, and George, too, was "smitten." According to some accounts, they became engaged in 1906, while George was at West Point.

In any event, while at the Academy, George was apparently thinking about marriage. He wrote in his diary, "Should a man get married, he must be just as careful to keep his wife's love as he was to get it. He must always love her and never adopt the attitude of now that I've got you, I can take you for granted. Don't do that, ever."

After George graduated from West Point, he and Beatrice were married on May 26, 1910, on a beautiful spring day, in the Beverly Farms Episcopal Church near Boston, Massachusetts. Some friends and relatives said Beatrice Patton was marrying beneath her. Her father owned the famous American Woolen Company and was very distinguished in his own right. Although George Patton was only an army second lieutenant, he had no need to be ashamed of his own aristocratic background. But his background was that of the West and hers the East. However, as time went on the distance from East to West seemed to make very little difference.

Beatrice Patton knew how ambitious her husband was. She did everything she could to encourage him. She once said, "There is no career except that of a minister's wife in which a woman can be such a help, or such a detriment, to her husband as that of an army wife. She lives practically at his place of business and sees his associates daily. Her reputation begins at her first post and sticks to her as closely as her skin until she dies. I have known several able officers to be ruined absolutely by malicious, gossipy wives."

Most biographers have spoken about the loving relationship of the Pattons. He wrote to her every day when they were separated by war. She wrote, "...love grows stronger and closer, bigger and finer, and more esential with each year that passes. Especially, if it's the only love you ever had."

The Pattons in an authenticated photo of unknown date. Thanks to the Third Cavalry Museum, Fort Worth, Texas.

Chapter Eight

SABER GEORGE

So, George Patton started his professional life with a loving wife and assignment to Fort Sheridan, Illinois, as a cavalry officer. His abilities were soon recognized. At the time there was still much glamor attached to the cavalry. Soon he became known as a Hell for Leather Man. In 1911 he was transferred to Fort Myer, Virginia, where he was detailed to design a new cavalry saber.

For much of its life the cavalry had been using a saber which was a "curved hacking tool," as Patton described it. Patton had the unusual opportunity to go to France in 1913, where he studied saber methods and horsemanship at the French Cavalry School.

Using the knowledge he had acquired at the

French school, Patton transformed the American cavalry saber into an efficient attack weapon with a straight blade. He was so deeply involved in this project that he came to be known as "Saber George," his first nickname.

Transferred to the Mounted Service School at Fort Riley, Kansas, he became the first "Master of the Sword." This position called for him to rewrite completely the training regulations under which the cavalry operated. Strangely, the same young man who, at eleven, could not even read or write could, a few years later, carry out with distinction such a difficult assignment.

Chapter Nine

MILITARY OLYMPICS

In 1912, young Patton had another opportunity that brought him new experience, new travel and new maturity. He was the first American army officer to take part in the Military Olympics, held that year in Stockholm, Sweden. He was to take part in the Pentathlon, a competition consisting of five events, each one scored individually, with the highest combined score winning.

Patton had worked hard to prepare and felt confident that he could win. Some of that confidence was dampened when he came out only twenty-seventh in pistol shooting. This was a strange result, because only the day before in practice he had shot a new world record in the event.

However, the low score was probably his own fault. Patton insisted on using a regulation military .38 caliber revolver, which the rules permitted. However, most other entrants chose a .22 caliber weapon. When the heavier gun was fired, it tore out chunks of the target bullseye. Patton had apparently scored most of his shots in the bullseye, but the judges had no way of telling, so they scored a miss.

In the other events of the Pentathlon, George did well. He won first place in fencing, giving the French champion his only defeat. He placed second in swimming, third in cross-country riding, but because of his low score in marksmanship, his final score was fifth in the Pentathlon. It was said at the time that if the pistol shooting score had been differently graded, he would have won first place.

Opposite, Patton's West Point track record proved invaluable as he prepared for the Military Olympics in 1912. Following pages, spectators in the stands at the Olympics at Stockholm, Sweden, witnessed a speedy George Patton as he competed in the Pentathlon.

Chapter Ten

ON TO MEXICO

In 1915 George Patton joined the Eighth Cavalry at Fort Bliss and then was sent to Sierra Blanca, Texas. In a letter to Beatrice in September, 1915, Patton proudly reported that his troops in the regimental review all drew out sabers based on his design.

At about this time affairs in Mexico had become so confused that they threatened the U.S. border. Mexican leader Pancho Villa had turned into an outlaw fighting the central Mexican government. Some outlaws, generally thought to have been Villa's men, shot a group of Americans at Chihuahua, and others crossed the New Mexican border, raided the U.S. town of Columbus, New Mexico and killed U.S. citizens there.

There was such outrage in the U.S. that President Woodrow Wilson ordered famed American General John J. Pershing to enter Mexico and capture Villa dead or alive.

Itching for war adventures, George Patton joined Pershing as his aide de camp. In May, 1916, Pershing's forces were attempting to locate Villa's bodyguard, "General" Julio Cardenas, near the town of Rubio. Lieutenant Patton was told that Cardenas's mother lived on a ranch called San Miguelito. Patton reconnoitered the ranch layout but left without finding Cardenas.

On May 14, Pershing was told that his troops had a shortage of corn, and he instructed Patton to go to nearby haciendas to purchase supplies. He took three Dodge cars, a corporal, six privates and a civilian interpreter.

The search for corn was not very successful, but Patton learned that Cardenas might be hiding out at his mother's ranch and that he might be guarded by as many as twenty men. The motorized outfit headed for the ranch and halted out of sight. Patton stationed his "motorized units" strategically around the hacienda.

Patton himself closed in on the ranch to observe it, just as three men dashed out on horseback. When they met part of Patton's force, they turned back toward the solitary Patton. General Pershing had been ordered not to make any first attack. However, his troops could return fire if fired upon.

The Mexicans did not know they were facing

the world's best shot and began to fire at Patton. Deliberately firing five rounds, Patton hit the leader, broke his arm and shot his horse. Reloading, he hit the next man's horse, which fell pinning the Mexican to the ground.

Patton waited for him to get free of the horse then killed him with a single shot. The third man galloped off and met some of Patton's men. The man Patton had wounded ran along the south wall of the hacienda grounds, returning the fire of all the Americans. When he stopped shooting, he raised his arm, apparently surrendering, then suddenly shot himself.

This man was identified as General Cardenas.

All the time this rapid action was going on an old man and a boy were skinning a steer. They did not bother to stop their work during the fray, and Patton and his men were careful not to harm them.

A search of the hacienda showed there were no other armed men present. Patton and his men strapped the three dead bandits, one to each of the Dodge cars, cut the telephone lines to Rubio and entered the town with the dead men displayed on the hoods like deer. They got safely through the town and arrived at Pershing's headquarters. He

Opposite, with Pershing in Mexico, Patton took part in what has been called the first military operation using motorized vehicles.

was delighted when he saw the "trophies" and from that time on called Patton his "Bandit."

On May 17, 1916, Patton wrote home to his wife, "... you are probably wondering if my conscience hurts me for killing a man. It does not. I feel about it just as I did when I got my first swordfish; surprised at my luck." He had already carved two notches into the grip of his Colt .45, proud to be a "blooded soldier."

In the official report of the hacienda incident, the assistant secretary of war declared "The Punitive Expedition into Mexico in 1916 in pursuit of Francisco Villa marked the real beginning of the use of motor transportation for the Army..." The newspapers had made much of the capture of Cardenas, and Patton was quoted as saying, "The motorcar is the modern warhorse." He had become a prophet, foretelling the mechanized warfare soon to come. He was to become the greatest commander in that new type of combat.

Chapter Eleven

THE PREHISTORIC PENNY

History records much of Patton's tremendous ambition and drive, of his intense concentration on succeeding in everything he was required to do. But little has been said about his sense of humor, which was certainly a part of his makeup, if in a rather unusual form.

While in Mexico, Patton and the men of the American force had become aware of the ancient ruins throughout much of Mexico and the many treasures they contained which had been left in them from prehistoric times. A good many of the Americans were amateur archeologists, or at least aware of the importance of these ancient leftovers.

Patton showed little interest in the significance of these artifacts, but he was interested in playing a joke on the ones who were interested.

He wrote to a friend, "There are some officers here very much interested in the Indian Ruins. They talk very learnedly about them. So yesterday I took some one-cent pieces and beat them upon a rock. Then I hid them in a ruin; they were soon found and caused great excitement. Fancy the men of the stone-age using money. You will see it in the next *Scientific American* or *National Geographic*. I enclose one of the coins which I made."

No record indicates that the hoax ever reached as far as the national magazines, but the prank does illustrate that Patton did not always have his mind on serious matters.

Chapter Twelve

TANKS AT LAST

As World War I drew closer to America, Patton returned to the U.S. On May 15, 1917, Patton was promoted to Captain. Three days later he sailed for Europe on the transport ship *Baltic* as part of General Pershing's headquarters organization of the American Expeditionary Forces.

Assigned to the tank corps, which was still in the planning stage, Patton was sent to the French Tank School and saw action at the Battle of Cambrai, when tanks were first used by the British on a large scale. In November, 1917, as the first and only American tank man, Patton organized and led the American tank center at Langres, France, and he received an appointment as major.

A 58-page report by Patton dated December 12, 1917, entitled Light Tanks, marked the beginning of an entirely new idea of warfare, and the entire planning of the country for armored war was based on it. Patton was responsible for writing all the first instructions for training U.S. army men in tank operations, as well as all the regulations regarding tanks. He even created the first arm patches worn by his armored corps.

As his grandfather had been before him, Patton was made a brigade commander. He was in charge of his newly formed tank group at the Battle of St. Mihiel in September, 1918, where they were all under fire. The enemy retreated in the face of Patton's well trained tank forces, which he commanded skillfully.

The Allies planned an offensive to drive the Germans out of the area of Meuse-Argonne in France. Patton's plan for using the American tanks in depth was accepted, and again the tanks performed extremely well. However, on September 23 Patton was severely wounded. He received the Purple Heart. For "conspicuous courage, coolness, energy and diligence in directing the advance of his unit" he was awarded the Distinguished Service Cross.

After the war he received the Distinguished Service Medal with a citation which read, "By his energy and judgment he rendered very valuable service in his organization and direction of the tank center at the Army Schools at Langres, and in the employment of Tank Corps troops in action, he displayed high military attainments, and marked adaptability in a form of warfare comparatively new to the American forces."

It was in this new form of warfare that Patton was later to be considered the greatest master.

Following pages, in World War I, Patton became the top expert in tank warfare. Here he is shown as a U.S. Tank Corps Lieutenant Colonel in front of a Renault tank, near Bourg, France, summer of 1918.

Chapter Thirteen

TANK RELIGION—A NEW DOCTRINE

After the war and after recovering from his wound, Patton hoped that the success of tanks in the war would lead to greatly increased attention and interest in them. He was assigned to lead the 304th brigade at Camp Meade Maryland. There he became reacquainted with Dwight D. Eisenhower. That association with various ups and downs was to continue in one way or another for the rest of his life.

Eisenhower wrote about Patton: "Among these men of the tank corps the one who interested me most, and whom I learned to like best, was a fellow named Patton. Colonel George S. Patton was tall, straight, and soldierly looking. His most noticeable characteristic was a high, squeaking voice, quite out of keeping with his bearing. He had two passions, the military service and polo. Side issues for George Patton were pleasure riding—he had a fine stable of good horses—and pistol shooting.

"From the beginning he and I got along famously. I did not play polo...but I was devoted to riding and shooting. Both of us were students of current military doctrine. Part of our passion was a belief in tanks—a belief derided at the time by others....We had started at Meade tactical and technical schools on this new weapon....We began to evolve what we thought to be a new and better tank doctrine."

The old military theory about the use of tanks, the one used in World War I, was that the tanks should move about fifty yards ahead of the foot soldiers, destroy machine gun nests and clear the way for the infantry. For this work tanks did not need to develop speed, only had to move ahead at about the three-mile-per-hour pace of a foot soldier.

Patton, Eisenhower and other young officers of the tank corps wanted a more spectacular role for tanks. They believed tanks should have great speed to dash ahead in large numbers and cause panic in enemy lines, make important breakthroughs in large areas and manage to encircle large segments of the enemy.

They were particularly interested in the tank developed by a man named Christie. To understand that tank better, they took it apart piece by piece and asked themselves if they could ever put it together again. They did.

They also experimented with their ideas. One day Eisenhower and Patton were working in the field on a military problem. A big tank had to drag three small tanks through a ravine by cable. The two officers were at the top of the slope waiting for the tanks when the cable snapped. Just past their faces it ripped like a huge razor, slashing bushes and saplings.

Later, Patton asked Ike: "Were you as scared as I was?"

"I was afraid to bring the subject up," Ike said. "We were certainly not more than five or six inches from sudden death."

With their careful experiments, the small group headed by Patton had become convinced that they were pioneering a device that could completely change warfare on land—a land-roving battleship. When they added the use of tanks to the accepted military theory, each time, also in theory, the tanks increased the prospect of victory.

The War Department did not go along with them. In time of peace the money for military forces is usually cut way back. After World War I the United States dropped a large part of its army and navy and kept only a skeleton force, as outlined in Congress' defense legislation of 1920. When the U.S. refused to spend the money to buy and develop the Christie tank, France and Great Britain also turned it down. So Christie sold it to the Germans, and it became the forerunner of the tank used in their famous Panzer divisions.

When the tank corps was made part of the infantry in another money-saving move, George went back to the cavalry.

Chapter Fourteen

WAITING FOR ANOTHER WAR

The wealth of the Pattons made it possible for them to indulge their interests. They had a fine sailing sloop and loved to sail in Salem Harbor, Massachusetts, where they had a handsome home. Beatrice was a fine sailor and won many races on her own. They once used all their sailing skills to rescue three boys from drowning in Salem harbor. While Beatrice managed the boat George swam to each boy separately and brought the three back to safety. He was given the silver Life Saving Medal of Honor by the U.S. treasury department.

Patton's interest in fine dining with influential friends and in all aspects of social life helped create the impression that he was a playboy. On one occasion Patton arrived at a dinner party in

When he was not at war, the Pattons were able to live a good and luxurious life, exemplified by this 1939 Cadillac, preserved at the Patton Museum, and other fine properties, such as their yacht.

full dress uniform. A drunken reserve colonel in the dining room saw him and remarked loudly, "That man's one of those all chicken, chicken on his shoulder and chicken in the heart."

Before George could raise a hand, Beatrice had attacked the man. The tiny wife knocked him down and pounded his head on the floor until George reached her and dragged her away. It was noted that both the Pattons had very short and violent tempers.

Of course, the playboy image was not really deserved. In addition to being a tank expert he was a great student of military tactics in general. He assembled one of the world's largest private collections of military volumes. He knew the campaigns of Lee, Grant, Frederick the Great and Napoleon by heart and could recite them from memory at length.

George Patton had one of the best formal educations of any U.S. officer, beginning with VMI and West Point. In 1934 he finished the Field Officers Course of training at Fort Riley, Kansas. He graduated with honors the next year from the Command and General Staff college at Fort Leavenworth, Kansas.

While at the Fort Leavenworth school he made very complete notes, which he loaned to Dwight Eisenhower who was at the school in 1936. When Eisenhower finished the course at the head of his class, he said that the Patton notebook had helped him greatly in his class standing.

From 1928 to 1931 Patton served in Washington, D.C., in the office of the chief of cavalry. He graduated from the Army War College in 1932, then served with the third cavalry at Fort Myer, Virginia, until 1935. Then he served with the General Staff in the Hawaiian islands for two years.

During the Hawaiian assignment, Patton gained experience in amphibious landing operations, and this knowledge helped him in future commands. Beatrice occupied some of her time in Hawaii by writing two books. One was a collection of Hawaiian fairy tales, written in French. This book added substantially to the preservation of Hawaiian culture.

One of the most interesting results of Patton's stay in Hawaii was connected with his study of the Japanese in the Pacific area. On the basis of his observations, Patton predicted in a paper he wrote that the Japanese would strike Pearl Harbor in Hawaii. He wrote, "The vital necessity to Japan of a short war and of the possession of its termination of land areas for bargaining purposes may impel her to take drastic measures. It is the duty of the military to foresee and prepare against the worst possible eventuality."

In less than five years his worst fears would be realized with the attack by Japan on Pearl Harbor.

Patton returned from Hawaii to assume command of the Fifth Cavalry at Fort Clark, Texas, and in 1938 was ordered to Fort Myer once again, to command the Third Cavalry.

During what seemed like a long period when nothing much was happening, Patton was practicing and learning about war operations most of the time. He had written and published in *Cavalry Journal* more than a dozen articles on new phases of warfare, based on his studies and experience.

Patton experimented with many new ideas and all the new kinds of equipment he could get his hands on. He had a plane set up for his personal study of the "enemy." He made some of the first experiments in talking from tank to tank by radio. Everything he studied convinced him further of the importance of great speed in attack, of quick communication among all the forces, of air warfare and mechanized ground forces, and, especially of always attacking, rather than holding back.

For him all of this was only waiting and preparing for the real thing, but the time of relative inactivity was about over with the possibility that America would soon be dragged into the Second World War.

Patton was a master of training troops for combat. He could take a group of raw recruits and have them shaped up and ready to fight in record time. One of the toughest of disciplinarians, he was known as "Flash Gordon" by his men.

Chapter Fifteen

THE WARHORSE STIRS

With the prospect of American entry into the largest of all wars, and especially with the unheard of success of Hitler's Panzer tank divisions as they overran Western Europe, the American army at last began to wonder where it had been all those years while Patton and others had been urging it to modernize.

In July, 1940, Patton was ordered to duty as a brigade commander of the Second Armored Division. The old tanks were covered with rust, but even worse, tons of red tape made it almost impossible to get anything done. Patton called on a unique source of materiel. He bought much-needed equipment from Sears, Roebuck.

In short order the old tanks were put in running order and much of the confusion cleared up. Next Patton was assigned as commanding officer of the Second Armored Division at Fort Benning, Georgia, in April 1941. In rapid time he developed the force into what one commentator called, "...the toughest, most feared outfit of the whole Army. Its men were proud to belong to it."

That success was scarcely a surprise. During his cavalry days Patton had developed a reputation of being one of the country's "toughest" and sometimes most profane officers. His men began to call him "Flash Gordon" because of the helmet he wore and the grim face he flashed out of tank turrets. He was also known as "Old-Blood-and-Guts," "Georgie," or the "Green Hornet".

As America's participation in the war drew closer, Patton was made commanding general of the First Armored Corps. Anticipating that they would be serving in the Sahara Desert, Patton shipped the entire armored unit to Indio, California, and organized the Desert Training Center there. There he taught American soldiers how to live and fight in temperatures that were even hotter than those of Africa in the Sahara.

According to one account, "Patton did not spare himself any discomforts. He got up at 5:00 in the morning, ate salt tablets and fruit juices with all his meals (to combat the heat) and on military problems only one gallon of water a day for both drinking and washing. He encouraged rather than discouraged a spirit of camaraderie between officers and men which was closer than could be found anywhere else in the Army."

Chapter Sixteen

CARRYING THE "TORCH"

The first American landings of World War II were to be carried out in North Africa under the general direction of General Eisenhower. On July 31, 1942, Patton was ordered to Washington to prepare for the invasion of Africa, as second under Eisenhower. Patton's forces were to land on the Atlantic beaches of Morocco. His training in Hawaii had included the use of armored vehicles supporting assault troops and other modern techniques of landing operations.

The landing plans were concealed under the code name of "Operation Torch." They included the transport of Patton's second armored division from Fort Benning, Georgia, through Hampton Roads at Norfolk, Virginia. From there they would have to face the wolf pack of German U-boats.

Navy forces under Admiral Hewitt managed to get them safely through by using decoy ships sent to Sierra Leone in West Africa.

With landings across 200 miles of western Morocco's coast under way, Patton was just about to get into his own landing craft when it was destroyed by enemy fire. Nevertheless, he carried on with his command and made the first U.S. landing on hostile soil during World War II. At Fedala, Morocco, Patton joined his men in the fox-holes and scattered outposts. Finally the forces were consolidated, and the United States gained control of most of Morocco.

The plan had been to have Operation Torch so overwhelming and such a surprise that little blood would be shed, and this was precisely what happened. Patton was even more successful in overcoming the pitfalls of an occupation of Morocco.

As Military Governor he managed to maintain American military authority without removing the French military presence, which had remained there. He worked hard to keep U.S. military authority operating with as little friction as possible alongside the French civil government. He also was effective in keeping the delicate balance of relations with the Sultan of Morocco.

Patton's personal diplomacy in Morocco emphasized stability and the status quo, assisted by displays of friendship and good will on his part. In Morocco he was at his diplomatic best, displaying

For his extraordinary record in routing the Germans in North Africa, Patton received many honors. Commander of North African operations, Dwight Eisenhower, and Patton met at Patton's headquarters near Tunis on March 16, 1943. After a long conference on military matters, Ike surprised Patton and his staff by suddenly pulling out the three stars of a major general and pinning them on the astonished Patton, his first official word of the promotion.

his charm and personal effervesence. His diplomatic role there was said to have been, "...sensitive, perceptive, thoughtful and versatile. In both military and diplomatic roles he exercised considerable self-control."

Patton's diplomacy drove a wedge between the puppet government at Vichy, France, set up by the Germans, and the French forces remaining in northwest Africa. President Roosevelt called Operation Torch and its aftermath the, "...turning point in the war against Nazi Germany."

Patton's forces remained in Morocco until the Germans made a breakthrough at Kasserine Gap in Tunisia in February, 1943. Patton then was sent to take charge there, where he rallied the Allied force and led it to victory at Maknassy, El Guettar and Gafsa. General Omar Bradley then took command in North Africa, while Patton took over the final training of American troops for an invasion of Sicily.

Chapter Seventeen

"THE SLAP HEARD 'ROUND THE WORLD"

The invasion of Sicily had been chosen as the first of the long steps in recovering Europe from the grip of Hitler's Germany. The Island of Sicily was the closest part of Europe to the Allied forces in Africa. It was a natural choice as a stepping-stone to the mainland of the continent.

General Patton supervised the landing of the Seventh Army in Sicily from a headquarters ship and then landed and entered into that campaign with his usual determination. It is generally believed that Sicily would not have been conquered in thirty-eight days had it not been for his driving force.

However, this driving force had apparently taken a toll of the general's nerves. On August 3, 1943, Patton visited the 15th evacuation hospital

Opposite, on July 11, 1943, General Patton went ashore at Gela, Sicily, from his command, as shown in this army photo. His lightning capture of Sicily amazed the experts but took a heavy toll of his nerves and ended in a period of near disgrace.

on Sicily. He talked with, praised and encouraged wounded patients of the first medical battalion. Then a medical corps colonel made the following report about Patton's *Mistreatment of Patients in Receiving Tents:*

Lt. Gen. George S. Patton, Jr., came into the tent with the commanding officer and other medical officers. The general spoke to the various patients in the receiving tent and especially commended the wounded men. Then he came to Pvt. Kuhl who had been brought to the facility suffering from exhaustion and malaria and asked him what was the matter. The soldier replied, "I guess I can't take it." The general immediately flared up, cursed the soldier, called him all types of a coward, then slapped him across the face with his gloves and finally grabbed the soldier by the scruff of his neck and kicked him out of the tent. The soldier was immediately picked up by corpsmen and taken to a ward tent. There he was found to have a temperature of 102.2 degrees F...

Patton continued his inspection of the tent and came to another soldier, a veteran of four years who had gone to pieces when his buddy was killed, and the report continues that the soldier:

...who was sitting huddled up and shivering. When asked what his trouble was, the man replied, "It's my nerves. I can't stand the shelling anymore." He was still sobbing. The General then yelled at him, "Your nerves, hell; you are just a [profanity] coward, you yellow [profanity.]" He then slapped the man and said, "Shut up that [profanity] crying. I won't have these brave men here who have been shot at seeing a yellow bastard sitting here crying." He then struck the man again, knocking his helmet liner off and into the next tent. He then turned to the admitting officer and yelled, "Don't admit this yellow bastard: there's nothing the matter with him. I won't have the hospitals cluttered up with these [profanity] who haven't got the guts to fight." He then turned to the man again, who was managing to sit at attention though shaking all over and said, "You're going back to the front lines and you may get shot and killed, but you're going to fight. If you don't, I'll stand you up against a wall and have a firing squad kill you on purpose. In fact," he said, reaching for his pistol, "I ought to shoot you myself you [profanity] whimpering coward." As he left the tent the general was still yelling back at the receiving officer....Nurses and patients attracted by the shouting and cursing came from adjoining tents and witnessed this disturbance. The deleterious effects of such incidents upon the wellbeing of patients, upon the professional morale of hospital staffs, and upon the relationshiop of patient to physician are incalculable. It is imperative that immediate steps be taken to prevent a recurrence of such incidents.

When General Brenton Wallace interviewed a medical officer who had witnessed the slapping of the patient, the general had an entirely different version of the incident. He wrote, in part:

As for the so-called "slapping incidents:" General Patton made frequent visits to the hospitals to see that the wounded were being properly cared for. One day he visited a large hospital in Sicily when he commanded the Seventh Army. As he came to the last ward, having been much distressed by the sights he had seen of the severely wounded and how bravely they were bearing up, he saw suddenly a young soldier sitting on the edge of his cot, apparently crying. Patton went over and said, "What's wrong, soldier, are you hurt?"

Without rising, but burying his face in his hands, the soldier whimpered, "Oh, no, I'm not hurt, but, oh, it's terrible—terrible—boo-hoo-hoo."

With that the general, disturbed after seeing all the badly wounded and mutilated soldiers, commanded, "Stand up."

The soldier got to his feet and the general slapped him across the neck with his gloves, which he was carrying, and said, "Why don't you act like a man instead of a damn sniveling baby? Look at these severely wounded soldiers not complaining a bit and as cheerful as can be, and here you are, a [profanity] crybaby."

I was told by the medical officers that it was the best thing that could have happened to the boy and that he was discharged from the hospital in less than a week, perfectly normal and well.

The report eventually reached the high command at Eisenhower's headquarters.

Chapter Eighteen
EISENHOWER'S REPRIMAND

General Patton received a letter from General Eisenhower, dated August 17, 1943, personally delivered by headquarters chief surgeon, General F.A. Blesse. The letter read:

I am attaching a report which is shocking in its allegations against your personal conduct. I hope you can assure me that none of them is true; but the detailed circumstances communicated to me lead me to the belief that some ground for the charges must exist.

I am well aware of the necessity for hardness and toughness on the battlefield. I clearly understand that firm and drastic measures are at times necessary in order to secure the desired objective. But this does not excuse brutality, abuse of the sick, nor exhibition of uncontrollable temper in front of subordinates.

In the two cases cited in the attached report, it is not my present intention to institute any formal investigation. Moreover, it is acutely distressing to me to have such charges as these made against you at the very moment when an American Army under your leadership has attained a success of which I am extremely proud. I feel that the personal services you have rendered the United States and the Allied cause during the past weeks are of incalculable value; but nevertheless, if there is a very considerable element of truth in the allegations accompanying this letter, I must so seriously question your good judgment and your self-discipline as to raise serious doubts in my mind as to your future usefulness.

I am assuming, for the moment, that the facts in the case are far less serious than appears in this report, and that whatever truth is contained in these allegations reports an act of yours when, under the stress and strain of winning a victory, you were thoughtless rather than harsh. Your leadership of the past few weeks has, in my opinion, fully vindicated to the War Department and to all your associates in arms my own persistence in upholding your pre-eminent qualifications for the difficult task to which you were assigned.

Nevertheless, you must give to this matter of personal deportment your instant and serious consideration to the end that no incident of this character can be reported to me in the future, and I may continue to count upon your assistance in military tasks.

In Allied Headquarters there is no record of the attached report or of my letter to you, except in my own secret files. I will expect your answer to be sent to me personally and secretly. Moreover, I strongly advise that, provided that there is any semblance of truth in the allegations in the accompanying report, you make in the form of an apology or other such personal amends to the individuals concerned as may be within your power, and that you do this before you submit your letter to me.

No letter that I have been called upon to write in my military career has caused me the mental anguish of this one, not only because of my long and deep personal friendship for you but because of my admiration of your military qualities, but I assure you that conduct such as described in the accompanying report will not be tolerated in this theater no matter who the offender may be.

Chapter Nineteen

"KICK HIM WHILE HE'S DOWN"

After hearing about the affair, Beatrice Patton wrote, "The deed is done and the mistake made, and I'm sure Georgie is sorrier and has punished himself more than anyone could possibly realize....I just hope they won't kick him to death while he's down." Nevertheless, the public and press were to do plenty of kicking.

A good many highly placed members of the press had heard of the slapping affair. Some of them went to Eisenhower, who told them what he had done, and because of the war situation and the great need for Patton's leadership, they did not make the reports public.

More than three months later, noted radio commentator and newspaper columnist Drew Pearson suddenly made the story public in what he called a scoop. His account caused a sensation. Some members of Congress called for Patton to be dismissed. One even compared him to Hitler. Eisenhower was accused of covering the whole thing up.

General Patton did offer a kind of apology, merely explaining what he had done. In his diary he had written after Pearson's comments, "I had been expecting something like this to happen for some time because I am sure that it would have been much better to have admitted the whole thing to start with, particularly in view of the fact that I was right in what I did."

At another time Patton told reporters, "I do a lot of human things people don't give me credit for and I'm not as big a [profanity] as a lot of people think. The commander of invading troops is under great tension and may do things he later regrets." Perhaps that was as close to an apology as he could manage.

Actually, the general did not believe there was any real "sickness" in what was called shell shock, or battle fatigue. He simply felt that those who were thought to be suffering in that way were covering up for cowardice. For Patton the war was not an ordeal; it was a fulfilment of his destiny, of all he had worked for and studied as a military man. It was a challenge to manhood, and only cowards would not fight. What appeared to be a brutal act was, for Patton, simply helping soldiers to overcome cowardice.

Of course, General George Patton did go on to other spectacular victories and made great contributions to both the war and the peace. But the matter of the "slap heard 'round the world" continued to haunt him, and it formed a cloud around his place in history.

Chapter Twenty

THE SPEEDY THIRD

General Patton was removed from his command of the Seventh Army. He was left in Sicily on occupation duty and had no part in the invasion of Italy. This in spite of the fact that his victories in Sicily put the Allies in a position to invade Italy. The slapping incident was not the only matter to cloud his next appointment.

General Eisenhower wrote, "George Patton loved to shock people. Anything that popped into his mind came promptly out of his mouth, especially if it was bizarre....He loved to shake members of a social gathering by exploding a few rounds of outrageous profanity." Eisenhower also told of an incident in England when Patton said "...that after the war was over, Britain and America would have to rule the world and other nations

General Patton was the world's master of tank warfare, beating the Germans, the previous masters, at every turn, using such U.S. equipment as this Sherman tank, preserved at the Patton Museum of Cavalry and Armor at Fort Knox, Kentucky.

would have to conform." This was reported in the press, and Eisenhower was urged to discipline Patton.

With so many people opposed to Patton, Eisenhower felt that he could not put him in command of the troops which would invade France on D-Day. General Omar Bradley was chosen, instead of Patton.

However, Patton helped in the preparations for the invasion of Europe by the Allies.

After D-Day, On August 1, 1944, Patton, now in command of the Third Army, darted into action. In only 26 days his troops advanced fifty miles. By contrast, British commander Field Marshall Bernard Montgomery was only able to push the Germans back ten miles in fifty-five days. Patton and his army continued to rush forward, attacking the Germans across a huge area of 200 miles in only ten more days. Montgomery had moved forward only twenty miles in sixty-six days.

The great German Seventh Army appeared to be trapped between Patton and Montgomery. The British and American armies were separated by only twelve miles. The Third Army had all the men and equipment they needed to race ahead to the French town of Falaise and attempt what might have become one of the greatest victories in history, trapping the Germans and taking them as prisoners. Then headquarters ordered Patton to halt.

*On their knees, Patton and Major General James A. Van Fleet,
examine a map of the front, April 26, 1945.*

It was later thought that in order to please the British, the commanders wanted Montgomery to close the gap. Instead Montgomery failed to reach Falaise in time, and most of the German army escaped. Military historians are still debating about who was at fault in this.

The Third Army played important roles in many of the battles in France and Germany, especially in the relief of the Allies at the town of Bastogne and the defeat of the Germans in the Battle of the Bulge. Patton's forces captured Trier on March 1, 1945, captured most of the valley of the Rhine River, then crossed the Rhine and dashed across Germany. The Third Army advanced thirty miles a day. It is difficult to imagine the millions of problems involved in moving an army of 500,000 men with all their equipment and supplies for such a distance every day. This would be a challenging test even with no obstacles in the way. It is even more difficult to imagine how such an advance could have been made in the face of enormously strong enemy forces making an all-out effort to hold them back.

One of the general's few failures occurred in March, 1945. He ordered a tank force to race for sixty miles inside enemy lines to reach Hammelburg. His son-in-law was being held there as a prisoner. The raid was not a success.

By April 11, 1945, Patton's Third Army was nearing the border of Czechoslovakia. The Czech

capital of Prague was scarcely twenty-four hours away. The Russian forces were driving toward Prague from the east. Patton desperately called on Eisenhower to let his army move ahead and capture Prague before the Russians. He was commanded to hold back, and the Russians captured the capital city of Czechoslovakia.

Despite being denied their final triumph, Patton and his Third Army had inflicted 1,443,888 casualties on the enemy. By contrast, the Third Army's casualties were 160,692. They had taken 1,280,688 prisoners of war and had destroyed 801 pillboxes and bunkers in the Maginot and Siegfried lines, along with 648 enemy tanks. In doing all this they had liberated 81,522 square miles of territory.

Opposite, waiting for the Commander in Chief, General Eisenhower, Patton and his staff stand outside his headquarters at Etain, France, September 30, 1945, his faithful dog Willie at his side.

Chapter Twenty-One

POLITICS! POLITICS! POLITICS!

Why had matters been taken out of Patton's hands? Before the Allies invaded Italy and France, Hitler and Mussolini held most of Europe, but Hitler's terrible attack on Russia had failed. The Russians were only slowly regaining their strength. The British had held out against all the bombings of their homeland, but years of fighting had taken their toll. America was sending vast amounts of supplies and huge military forces to England. However, America was occupied on two fronts, with war still raging in the Pacific.

It was not at all certain that the British and Americans alone could recapture all of Europe, take Germany and overcome Hitler, especially while the Americans were so occupied in the Pacific.

All this was in the minds of the British and American leaders when, in January, 1943, Roosevelt, Churchill and Stalin had met at Teheran in Iran. At that time it seemed that the forces of all three nations—America, Britain and Russia—would be needed to conquer Hitler. The three leaders agreed that their forces would coordinate their attacks on Germany. They also agreed that each country would occupy and control certain areas of Germany.

As the Allied invasion continued, Patton and the other forces had reached a point where they probably could have taken most of Germany and much of the other areas of Eastern Europe which the Germans had conquered. General Eisenhower was critized bitterly for holding back, for not taking the German capital of Berlin and for letting the Russians have that honor. He was also faulted for refusing to let Patton occupy Prague.

However, President Roosevelt had made it perfectly clear to Ike that he must honor the agreements made at Teheran. So, the Allied forces held back; the Russians took Berlin and Prague, and Eastern Europe has been in their hands ever since.

From the standpoint of the Western World, it now appears that this was one of the worst mistakes that could have been made. At the time, though, the Allies had given the Russians their word, and they thought they could trust the Russians.

Three of the most important leaders of the free world met in Germany on July 28, 1945, for an important conference less than two months before World War II ended in Germany. Left to right, Commander-in-Chief Dwight D. Eisenhower, General George S. Patton, Jr., President of the United States, Harry S. Truman

Neither Eisenhower nor Patton trusted the Russians. Eisenhower had made this plain many years before. If Patton had had his way, he said he would have pushed the Russians all the way back to Moscow.

Historians probably will never agree on what should have been done or what might have been possible.

However, the war came to an end. Germany surrendered unconditionally, and the Allies and the Russians settled down to occupying the territories they held.

As soon as fighting in Europe was over Patton desperately wanted to take part in the war against Japan. Apparently, though, with General MacArthur in full stride in the Pacific, the U.S. leaders did not want to have "two prima donnas" in the Pacific war at one time.

So General Patton was assigned to be the military governor in the Bavarian sector of Germany. Eisenhower wanted to root out all Nazi control in Germany as quickly as possible. Patton appeared to be more concerned with helping the common people of Germany recover from the war. He left a number of Nazi civilian leaders in power in Bavaria because he said they were needed to keep some kind of order in the country and prevent starvation.

When criticized for this, once again Patton "shot off his mouth," called the press all kinds of names and made himself a target for the press and those who felt differently. As one writer put it, Patton continued to be the "...bullheaded four- star general who fought his superior officers, yellow-belly GI's, Washington politicians, the American press, not to mention field Marshall Rommell, Field Marshal Montgomery, the United States Congress, and other battlefield representatives of the Hun."

Finally he was removed from his post in Bavaria and assigned to the Fifteenth Army, which was to be occupied with minor tasks, in Patton's opinion.

Patton considered resigning to write his memoirs. He asked for a month's leave of absence to go home and ponder his next moves. The day before he was to leave for the U.S. he decided to go on a pheasant hunt. His car was struck by a truck, and the great general was paralyzed. Many writers have said how ironic it must have seemed to him while he lay conscious but unable to move that a man who survived two world wars and severe wounds was finally laid low by a traffic accident.

General George Patton lingered for twelve days in a military hospital in Heidelberg, Germany, and died in his sleep on December 21, 1945.

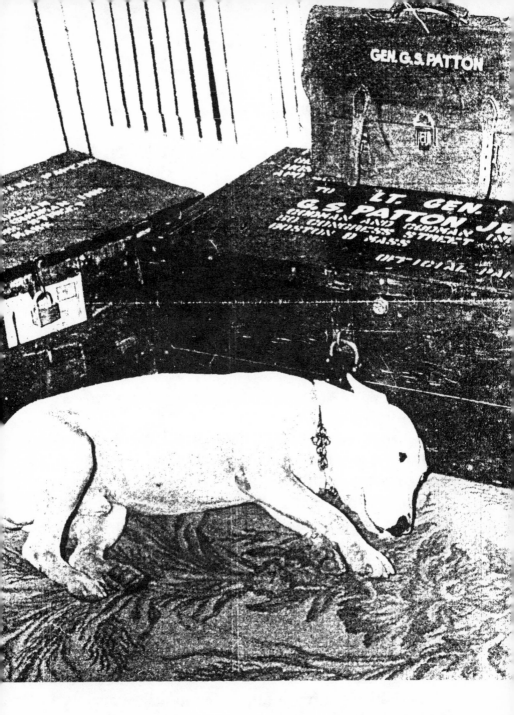

After his master's death, a lonesome dog, Willie, waits for transportation home, as shown courtesy of Life Magazine from the January 14, 1946, issue.

Chapter Twenty-Two

COMPLEX AND CONTROVERSIAL

Most of the writings about George Patton center around the man of action, the bold general, the driving ambitious man who would appear to go to almost any length to win. There was, however, another side to that bold general with the harsh demanding voice, the general feared by the Germans more than any other, more, perhaps than another side, almost a second personality. Some researchers have even concluded that an early accident affected his brain and influenced all of his later thoughts and actions.

One of his German opponents called Patton, "...a 16th century man—a romantic warrior, lost in contemporary times."

Patton wrote daily letters to his wife, Beatrice, sometimes twice a day if there were something important to tell her. In one of those letters he wrote, "I love you so, Bea....I am not so hellish young and it is not spring, yet still I love you just as much as if we were 22 again on the baseball grandstand at West Point the night I graduated."

In another letter he wrote on October 7, 1916, after he was badly burned when a gasoline lantern exploded in his face: "I love you with all my heart and would have hated worst to have been blinded because I could not have seen you."

Patton was noted for his fiery speeches to his men, but he also wrote poetry and planned to have a book of his poetry published after his death. In his letters to Beatrice, he often included a poem he had written.

Many of his poems indicated that he was not fond of battle for battle's sake but for the chance to prove over and over again that he was a real man. The following is one of the many poems he wrote which help to demonstrate both sides of his character:

THE MOON AND THE DEAD

The roar of the battle languished,
The hate from the guns was still,
While the moon rose up from a smoke cloud,
And looked at the dead on the hill.
Pale was her face with anguish,

Wet were her eyes with tears,
As she gazed on the twisted corpses,
Cut off in their earliest years.
Some were bit by the bullet
Some were kissed by the steel,
Some were crushed by the cannon,
But all were still, how still!
The smoke wreaths hung in the hollows,
The blood stink rose in the air;
And the moon looked down in pity,
At the poor dead lying there.
Light of their childhood's wonder,
Moon of their puppy love,
Goal of their first ambition,
She watched them from above.
Yet not with regret she mourned them,
Fair slain on the field of strife,
Fools only lament the hero,
Who gives for faith his life.
She sighed for the lives extinguished,
She wept for the loves that grieve,
But she glowed with pride on seeing
That manhood still doth live.
The moon sailed on contented,
Above the heaps of slain,
For she saw that manhood liveth,
And honor breathes again.

His critics said that George Patton had no
romance in his soul, that he only wanted "war and
the good life." Yet one of his fondest dreams, a

dream he never realized, was that someday he and Beatrice might sail around the world in their sixty-foot schooner, appropriately called the *When and If.*

Another side of his talent was shown by the fact that he helped to design that schooner, which both the Pattons loved so much.

In 1943, before some of Patton's greatest triumphs, the journal *Current Biography* carried a short life of the general. That article told how Beatrice had learned to wait at home while the general was at war and how she had written a ten-point code for wives who could only wait, as she did in their beautiful farmhouse at Hamilton, Massachusettes, and pray and work for peace.

The article concluded by an observation which proved strangely prophetic but not quite accurate: "Mrs. Patton has need of rules, since the general has often told her of his premonition that he would be killed in action. This suits his love of the dramatic—death will come during battle, and it will be glorious."

For one of America's greatest military strategists, a man who often had led his troops in the heat of battle, for "roaring, gimlet-eyed, two-gun General Patton," for "one of America's foremost commanders," that prophecy was not to come true. Death came in a different and far less glorious manner.

HIGHLIGHTS

1885, November 11, Born at San Gabriel, California

1896, Enters Classical School for Boys

1903-1904, Attends Virginia Military Academy

1904, Enters U.S. Military Academy at West Point

1905, Made to repeat first year of Military Academy

1909, June 11, Graduates from Military Academy

1910, May 26, Marries Beatrice Ayer

1912, First American to take part in Military Olympics

1913, Studies swordsmanship in France

1915, Joins 8th Cavalry at Fort Bliss

1916, March 13, crosses Mexican border with Pershing

1916, May 14, Captures Cardenas, inaugurates mechanized warfare

1917, May 18, Sails for France and World War I

1917, November, Organizes American tank force at Langres, France

1917, December 12, Publishes first instruction manual on tank warfare

1918, September, Under fire at St. Mihiel

1918, September 22, Wounded at Battle of Meuse-Argonne

1919, At Camp Meade

1924, At Command and General Staff College, Leavenworth, Kansas

1928-1931, Assigned to Office of Chief of Cavalry at Washington, D.C.

1932, Graduates from Army War College

1935-1937, Assigned to Army General Staff, Hawaii, studies landing operations

1940, July, Brigade commander 2nd Armored Division

1941, April, Commands 2nd Armored Division, Fort Benning, Georgia

1941, November, Commands 1st Armored Corps in U.S. desert exercises

1942, July 31, to Washington to prepare for African invasion

1942-1943, Invades Morocco, is military governor there

1943, February, Victories in North Africa

1943, August, Conquers Sicily, the "slap heard 'round the world"

1943, August 17, Eisenhower sends private letter with reprimand for slap incident, calls for apologies

1944, August 1, Patton begins push of Third Army in France

1945, April 11, Ordered to halt push on Prague, Czechoslovakia

1945, October, Removed as Military Governor of Bavaria

1945, December 21, General George S. Patton dies in his sleep

SOME SOURCES OF FURTHER INFORMATION

Allen, Colonel Robert S.,
   Lucky Forward: The History of Pattons' Third U.S. Army, Vanguard, 1947
Ayer, Fred, Jr.,
   Before the Colors Fade: Portrait of a Soldier, George S. Patton, Jr., with a Foreword by General of the Army Omar N. Bradley, Houghton Mifflin, 1964
Blumenson, Martin,
   ——-, *Patton: The Man Behind the Legend, 1885-1945,* William Morrow, 1985
   ——-, *The Patton Papers, 1885-1940,* Houghton Mifflin, 1972
   ——-, *The Patton Papers, 1940-1945,* Houghton Mifflin, 1974
Blumenson, Martin and James L. Stokesbury,
   Masters of the Art of Command, Houghton Mifflin, 1975
Bradley, Omar N.,
   A Soldier's Story, Henry Holt, 1951
Codman, Colonel Charles R.,
   Drive, Little, Brown, 1957

Many memories of General George S. Patton and the wars he fought are preserved at the Patton Museum of Cavalry and Armor at Fort Knox, Kentucky.

WHAT HE SAID

Author's note: The following quotations were all spoken or written by Patton. They have been recorded in various sources. General George Patton's own words describe him and show his thinking far better, perhaps, than the words of friends, relatives, colleagues or historians. We are indebted to the Patton Museum of Cavalry and Armor and the Museums of Fort Sheridan for supplying materials.

It has come to my attention that a very small number of soldiers are going to the hospitals on the pretext that they are nervously incapable of combat. Such men are cowards, and they bring discredit to the Army and disgrace to their comrades...who endure the dangers of battle, while they themselves use the hospitals as a means of escape.

I am convinced that my actions in this case [the slapping incident] were entirely correct, and that had other officers had the courage to do likewise, the shameful excuse of battle fatigue instead of cowardice would have been infinitely reduced.... General Joyce, to whom I talked about the Drew Pearson incident the slapping incident remarked, "George, just tell them the exact truth in these words; 'I had been dealing with heroes. I saw two men whom I thought were cowards. Naturally, I was not too gentle with them.'" This is exactly true, but there is no use in repeating it....The thing which hurts me is that as far as I can see, my side of the case has never been heard. It is like taxation without representation....If the fate of the only successful general in the war depends on the statement of a discredited writer like Drew Pearson, we are in a bad fix....for every man that I have criticized in this Army, I have probably stopped, talked to, and complimented a thousand, but people are prone to remember ill usage more than to recall compliments.

It is rather a commentary on justice when an Army commander has to soft soap a skulker to placate the timidity of those in command above...

I will resign when I have finished this job, which will be not later than December 26th. I hate to do it, but I have been gagged all of my life and whether they appreciate it or not, Americans need some honest men who dare to say what they think, not what they think people want them to say.

I could have taken Berlin if I had been allowed.

The Russians have a lot of new heavy tanks of which they are very proud. The marshal asked me how I liked them. I said that I did not and we had quite an argument. Apparently I am the first person ever to disagree with him.

At the dinner I stated that in my opinion Germany was so completely blacked out that so far as military resistance was concerned, they were not a menace and that what we had to look out for was Russia. This caused a considerable furor.

I believe that Germany should not be destroyed, but rather should be rebuilt as a buffer against the real danger, which is Russia and its Bolshevism.

I am firmly convinced that we must have a universal system of training. The only hope for a peaceful world is a powerful America with the adequate means to instantly check aggres-

sors. Unless we are so armed and prepared, the next war will probably destroy us. No one who has lived in a destroyed country can view such a possiblity with anything except horror.

Many of us have never experienced the God-sent ecstasy of unbridled wrath. We have never felt our eyes screw up, our temples throb, and have never had the red mist gather in our sight. But, we expect that a man shall, in an instant...divest himself of all restraint, of all caution, and hurl himself upon the enemy....Therefore, you must school yourself to savagery. You must imagine how it will feel when your sword hilt crashes into the breastbone of your enemy. You must picture the wild exaltation of the mounted charge when the lips are drawn back into a snarl and the voice cracks with passion. At one time, you must be both a wise man and a fool. A young soldier upon being asked by Napoleon what he desired in recompense for an heroic act said, "Sire, the Legion of Honor," to which Napoleon replied, "My boy, you are over young for such an honor." The soldier again said, "Sire, in your service, we do not grow old." This story is as true as it is tragic. Our men do not grow old. We must exploit their abilities and satisfy their longings to the utmost during the brief span of their existence. Surely, an inch of satin for a machine gun nest put out of action is a bargain not to be lightly passed up.

This "Blood and Guts" stuff is quite distasteful to me. I am a very severe disciplinarian because I know that without dis-

*cipline it is impossible to win battles, and that without dis-
cipline to send men into battle is to commit murder. [The
story has been told that Patton's men complained that he
meant "our blood, your guts," but that they would follow him
to hell, probably because of his personal courage.]*

*People ask why I swagger and swear, wear flashy uniforms
and sometimes two pistols. Well, I'm not sure whether or not
some of it isn't my own fault. However that may be, the press
and others have built a picture of me. So, now, no matter
how tired, or discouraged or really even ill I may be, if I don't
live up to that picture, my men are going to say, "the old
man's sick, the old son of a bitch has had it." Then their own
confidence, their own morale will take a big drop.*

*In any war, a commander, no matter what his rank, has to
send to certain death, nearly every day, by his own orders, a
certain number of men. Some are his personal friends. All
are his personal responsibility; to them as his troops and to
their families. Any man with a heart would like to sit down
and bawl like a baby, but he can't. So, he sticks out his jaw,
and swaggers and swears. I wish some of those pious sob
sisters at home could understand something as basic as that.*

*I believe that in war the good of the individual must be
subordinated to the good of the Army....To me, it is a never
ending marvel what our soldiers can do.*

It is interesting to note that everything for which I have been criticized in the handling of the Germans has subsequently been adopted by our Military Government. I stated that if we took all of the small Nazis out of every job, chaos would result, and it did. The Military Government the other day announced that from two to five percent of Nazis would be permitted to stay in government offices.

All Nazis are bad, but not all Germans are Nazis.

The point which I was and am still trying to bring out is that in Germany practically all or at least a very large percentage of the trades people, small businessmen, and even professional men, such as doctors and lawyers, were beholden to the Nazi party. Without the patronage of the Nazi party, they could not carry on their business and work at their professions. Therefore many of them were forced to give lip service to the party.

We could have arrived sooner but for the fact that if one flies over Russian-occupied territory they shoot at you. Nice friends....[Nice friend, indeed, as Patton further describes.] One form of securing testimony used by the Russians is to hang a man by his wrists with bandages so that they will not cut or leave marks. Then, two small incisions are made into the lower abdomen to allow a portion of the intestines to hang out. After the man has taken all he can stand without dying, he is cut down, the incisions are sewn up, and he is restored to health with the promise that the operation will not be repeated IF he does as he is told.

...when we were going along well and could easily have taken Berlin, Churchill asked Ike to do it. Ike replied by stating that it was Churchill's fault that the line had been established where it was. I believe that this was a great mistake on Ike's part because, had we taken the country to the Moldau River and Berlin we could have...prevented what I believe historians will consider a horrid crime...by letting the Russians take the two leading capitals of Europe.

If we have to fight them, [the Russians] now is the time. From now on, we will get weaker and they will get stronger.

We are turning over to the French several hundred thousand Prisoners of War to be used as slave labor in France. It is amusing to recall that we fought the Revolution in defense of the rights of man, and the Civil War to abolish slavery, and have now gone back on both principles.

Actually the Germans are the only decent people left in Europe. It's a choice between them and the Russians. I prefer the Germans.

Ike called up late and said that, "My American boss will visit you in the morning." I asked, "When did Mamie arrive?" Man cannot serve two masters.

Ike has to a high degree the "Messiah Complex" for which he can't be blamed since everybody bootlicks him except me.

INDEX

* Denotes Illustrations
Aberdeen, Scotland, 15
Abolition of Slavery, 107
Accident, traffic, 92
Africa, 63, 64, 65, 66, 67, 68
Africa, invasion of, 64, 65
Air warfare, 60
Alcalde (leader) of LA, 20
Allied Forces, 67, 68
Allied Headquarters, 76
Allied invasion, 89
Allies, 83, 85
Ambition, 45
America & Britain, rule the world, 81
American Expeditionary Forces, 47
American Indian agent, 20
American leader, 89
American press, 78, 92, 105
American Revolution, 15, 18, 107
American Tank center, 47
American Woolen Company, 31
Amphibious landing operations, 59
Apache Indians, 19
Apology, 76, 79
Archeologists, amateur, 45
Arm patches, 48
Armored warfare, 48, 49
Army letter, 27
Army Schools at Langres, 49
Army War College, 59
Army wife, 32
Atlantic beaches, 64
Aunt, 30
Aunts & Uncles, 18, 30
Automobile accident, 92
Automobiles, 7, 10, 11, 41, 42, 44, 57*, 92
Ayers, Beatrice (wife), 30, 31, 32, 40, 44, 56,
58, 59, 78, 95, 97
Ayers, Frederick, 30
Ayers, Frederick, Jr., 30
Ayers, Katherine, 30
"Baltic" (transport ship), 47
Bandit (Patton, Jr. nickname), 44
Bandits, 20
Baptism by fire, 10
Baseball grandstand, West Point, 95
Bastogne, Belgium, 85
Battle fatigue, 79, 102
Battle of Cambrai, 47
Battle of Gettysburg, 13
Battle of Saint Mihiel, 48
Battle of the Bulge, 85
Battle of Winchester, 12, 13
Bavaria (Germany), 91, 92, 106
Bavaria, policy in, 106
Bavarian sector of Germany, 91
Bavarian sector, Military Governor, 91
Berlin, Germany, 89, 103, 107
Beverly Farms Episcopal Church, 31
Bibliography, 100
Blesse, F. A., 74
"Blood-and-Guts, Old" (George Smith Patton,
Jr.), 22, 63, 105

"Blooded soldier", 44
Bolshevism, buffer against, 103
Bombing of Britian, 88
Boston, Massachusetts, 31
Bourg, France, 49
Braddock, Edward, 18
Bradley, Omar, 67, 83
Britain & America, rule the world, 81
British & American armies, 83
British bombings, 88
British leader, 89
British Prime Minister, 89
Broken arm, 27
Brutality, 75
Buffer against Bolshevism, 103
Bulge, Battle of the, 85
Cadillac (1939), 57*
California pioneer stock, 22
California, 19, 20, 22, 30
Cambrai, Battle of, 47
Camp Meade, Maryland, 52
Car accident, 92
Cardenas, Julio, 10, 41, 42, 44
Carranza, Venustiano, 9
Catalina Island, California, 30
Cavalry, 29, 33, 55, 59, 60
Cavalry Journal, 60
Cavalry, office of the chief of, 59
Cavalry officer, 29, 33
Challenge to manhood, 79
Character, 12, 95
Chicken remark, 58
Chihuahua, Chihuahua, Mexico, 40
Children, 13
Choctaw Indians, 19
Christie (tank designer), 53, 55
Christie tank, 53, 55
Chronology, 98-99
Churchill, Winston, 89, 107
Civil War, 12, 13, 14, 18, 21, 22, 107
Civilian leaders, Nazi, 91
Clark, Stephen Cutter, 26
Code for wives, ten-point, 97
Colt forty-five (.45), 44
Columbus, New Mexico, 9, 40
Command and General Staff college, 58
Commander of North African operations, 66*
Commander-in-Chief Allied Expeditionary
Forces, 87, 90*
Comments, 102, 103, 104, 105, 106, 107
Communications, 60
Compliments, 103
Conduct, personal, 70, 71, 72, 73, 74, 76
Confederate Brigadier General, 18
Confidence, men's, 105
Congress of the U.S., 79, 92
Controversial comments, 102, 103, 104, 105,
106, 107
Cover by Wesley Klug
Coverup, 79
Cowardice, 71, 79, 102
Cowards, 71, 102
Cross-country riding,

Current Biography, 97
Czechoslovakia, 85, 87
Czechoslovakia, capital, 87
D-Day, 83
Dates, important, 98-99
Death of Grandfather (paternal), 12
Death of Patton, 92, 97
Debts, repayment of, 23
Defense of human rights, 107
Demerits, West Point, 27
Description, 52, 53, 102
Desert Training Center, 63
Design, cavalry saber, 33
Destiny, fulfilment, 79
Disciplinarian, 61, 83, 105
Discipline, 83
Distinguished Service Cross, 48
Distinguished Service Medal with citation, 48
Distrust of Russians, 91
Dodge cars, 10, 11, 41, 42
Dog (Willie), 86*, 93*
Don (Spanish title), 20
Don Benito (Benjamin Davis Wilson), 20
Draft, military, 104
Dyslexia, 23, 24
Eastern Europe, 89
Ecstasy of wrath, 104
Education, 23, 24, 26, 58
Eisenhower, Dwight D., 52, 53, 54, 58, 64, 90*, 64, 66*, 73, 74, 78, 79, 81, 83, 87, 89, 107
Eisenhower, Mamie, 107
El Guettar, Tunisia, 67
El Pueblo de Nuestra Senora la Reina de Los Angles de Porciuncula (Los Angles, California), 20, 21
Engagement, 31
England, 81
Etain, France, 87
Europe, 47, 83
Europe, invasion of, 83
Exhaustion, 70
Experiments with tanks, 54
Failures, 85
Fairy tales, Hawaiian, 59
Falaise, France, 83, 85*
Family portrait, 16-17*
Father's educational theory, 24
Father, 16-17*, 21, 23, 24
Fedala, Morocco, 65
Fencing (sport), 37
Field Officers Course, 58
Fifth Cavalry, 60
Firing squad, 71
First Armored Corps, 63
First mechanized warfare, 10, 11, 42, 44
"Flash Gordon" (George Smith Patton, Jr.), 61, 63
Football, 27
Fort Benning, Georgia, 63, 64
Fort Bliss, Texas, 40
Fort Clark, Texas, 60
Fort Duquesne (Pennsylvania), 18
Fort Knox, Kentucky, 101, 82
Fort Leavenworth, Kansas, 58
Fort Myer, Virginia, 33, 59, 60
Fort Riley, Kansas, 34, 58
Fort Sheridan, Illinois, 33

Forty-five (.45) Colt revolver, 44
France, 33, 47, 83, 88, 107
France, invasion of, 83, 88
Frederick the Great, 58
Fredericksburg, Virginia, 15
French Cavalry School, 33
French Legion of Honor, 104
French Tank School, 47
French test, 27
Fulfilment of destiny, 79
Gafsa, Tunisia, 67
Gela, Sicily, 68
General Staff, 59
"Georgie" (George Smith Patton, Jr.), 63
German army escape, 85
German army, 66, 83
German capital, 89
German prisoners, 83
German Seventh Army, 83
German unconditional surrender, 91
German people, 106, 107
Germany (as a buffer against Bolshevism), 103
Glorification of war, 14
God, 13
Government, Military, 65, 91, 106
Graduation from West Point, 29, 31, 28
Graduation picture, 28*
Grandfather (maternal), 19, 20, 21, 22
Grandfather (paternal), 12, 14, 18
Grandfather, step (paternal), 18
Grandmother (maternal), 21
Grapes, 20
Great-grandfather (paternal), 13, 18
Great-great-grandfather (paternal), 15, 18
Great-great-grandmother (paternal), 18
Great-great-great-grandfather (paternal), 18
"Green Hornet" (George Smith Patton, Jr.), 63
Grey Ghost (John Mosby), 14
Guerrilla warfare, 9, 10
Halt orders, 83, 87, 89
Hamilton, Massachusettes, 97
Hammelburg, Germany, 85
Hampton Roads, Virginia, 64
Hawaii training, 64
Hawaiian culture, preservation, 59
Hawaiian fairy tales, 59
Hawaiian islands, 59
Heidelberg, Germany, 92
Held back, 83, 87, 89
"Hell for Leather Man" (George Smith Patton, Jr.), 33
Hereford, Margaret S. (grandmother), 21
Hewitt, Kent, 65
Highlights, 98-99
Hitler, Adolf, 62, 79, 88, 89
Hitler's Panzer tank divisons, 62
Hoaxes, 46
Holding back, 83, 87, 89
Horses, 10
Hospital visit, 70, 71, 72, 73
Humor, 45, 46
"Iliad" (poem), 24
Important dates, 98-99
Indian Ruins (Mexico), 46
Indian wars, 22
Indians, 19, 20, 22, 46
Indio, California, 63

Individuals in war, 105
Infantry, 55
Injuries, 27, 48, 92, 95
Interrogation, Russian, 106
Invasion by the Allies, 64, 65, 68, 69, 81, 83, 88, 89
Invasion of Africa, 64, 65
Invasion of Europe, 67, 68, 69, 81, 83, 88, 89
Invasion of France, 83, 88
Invasion of Germany, 89
Invasion of Italy, 81, 88
Invasion of Mexico, 9, 41
Invasion of Sicily, 67, 68, 69
Italy, invasion of, 81, 88
Jackson, Thomas Jonanthan "Stonewall", 13
Japan war against, 91
Japanese attack on Pearl Harbor, 59
Jesus Christ, 13
Jokes, 46
Joyce, William (Lord Haw-Haw), 102
Justice for Indians, 20
Kasserine Gap, Tunisia, 67
Killing, feelings after, 44
Klug, Wesley, Cover, 4
Kuhl, (Private), 70
Lake Vineyard, San Gabriel, California, 18
Landing on hostile soil, 65
Langres, France, 47, 49
Lantern explosion, 95
Leaders, Allied, 89
Lee, Robert E., 13, 14, 58
Legion of Honor, French, 104
Life Magazine, 93
Life Saving Medal of Honor (U.S. Treasury Department), 56
"Light Tanks" (report), 48
Loans, 22, 23
Los Angles, California, 20, 21
Loving relationship, 32
MacArthur, Douglas, 91
Maginot line, 87
Magna Charta signers, 15
Maknassy, Tunisia, 67
Malaria, 70
Manhood, challenge, 79
Marksmanship, 37
Marriage, 31
"Master of the Sword" (title), 34
Mayor of LA, 21
Meade tactical and technical schools, 53
Mechanized warfare, 10, 11, 42, 44, 60
Mechanized warfare, first, 10, 11, 42, 44
Media (press), 78, 92, 105
Memoirs, 92
Memorabilia, Civil War, 14
Mercer, Anna Gordon (great-great-grand-mother), 18
Mercer, Hugh (Great-great-great-grandfather), 18
Messiah Complex (Eisenhower's), 107
Meuse-Argonne (France), 48
Mexico, 7, 8, 9, 10, 40, 41, 42, 45,
Mexico, invasion, 9, 41
Military doctrine, 53
Military draft, 104
Military Government, 65, 91, 106
Military Governor of Bavarian sector, 91

Military Governor of Morocco, 65
Military Olympics, 35, 37, 38-39*
Military tactics, 58
Military theory, 53, 54
Military training, 61*, 104
Military training, universal, 104
Minister's wife, 31
"Mistreatment of Patients in Receiving Tents" (report), 70
Model T (car), 11
Moldau River, 107
Money, stone-age, 46
Montgomery, Bernard, 83, 85, 92
"Moon and the Dead, The" (poem), 95-96
Morale, 105
Morocco, Africa, 64, 65, 67
Morocco, Military Governor, 65
Morocco, Sultan of, 65
Mosby, John (Grey Ghost), 14
Moscow, Russia, 91
Mother, 16-17*, 21
Motorized warfare, 41, 42
Mounted Service School, 34
Mussolini, Benito, 88
Napoleon, 58, 104
National Geographic, 46
Nazi civilian leaders, 91
Nazi Germany, 67
Nazi members, 106
Nazi party, 106
Nazis, 67, 91, 106
New Mexico, 19
Newspapers, 78
Nicknames, 14, 22, 34, 44, 61, 63, 78, 105
Norfolk, Virginia, 64
North Africa, 63, 64, 65, 66, 67, 68
North American War, Fear of, 9
Occupation forces, 91
Office of the chief of Cavalry, 59
Old-Blood-and-Guts (George Smith Patton, Jr.), 22, 63, 105
Olympics, Military, 35, 37, 38-39*
"Operation Torch" (invasion of Africa), 64, 65, 67
Ordered to halt, 87, 83, 89
Pacific war front, 88, 91
Panzer tank divisons, 55, 62
Paralyzed, 92
Pasadena, California, 26
Pasadena High School, 26
Patches, arm, 48
Patton, Anna Mercer (great-great-grand-mother), 18
Patton, Anne Wilson (sister), 16-17*
Patton, Beatrice Ayers (wife), 30, 31, 32, 40, 44, 56, 58, 59, 78, 95, 97
Patton, George Smith (father), 16-17*, 21, 23, 24
Patton, George Smith (grandfather), 12, 14, 18
Patton, George Smith, Jr. (illustrations), cover, 8, 16-17, 21, 25, 28, 36, 38-39, 43, 50-51, 66, 69, 84, 86, 90
Patton, John Mercer (great-grandfather), 13, 18
Patton Museum of Cavalry and Armor, 4, 57, 82, 101*, 102
Patton, Robert (great-great-grandfather), 15,

18
Patton, Ruth Wilson Smith (mother), 16-17*, 21
Peace, 97, 104
Pearl-handled revolver 2-3*
Pearl Harbor, Hawaii, 59
Pearson, Drew, 78, 79, 102
Pentathlon, 35, 37, 38-39*
Pershing, John J., 9, 10, 41, 43*, 47
Personal conduct, 70, 71, 72, 73, 74, 76
Pet, 86*, 93*
Pickett, George E., 13
Pistol shooting, 35, 37, 53
Pistols, 2-3*, 105
Poem by Patton ("The Moon and the Dead"), 95-96
Poetry, 95-96
Poisoned Indian arrow, 19
Policy in Bavaria, 106
Policy, U.S. toward Russia, 107
Polo, 53
Pope, Alexander, 24
Prague, Czechoslovakia, 87, 89
Pranks, 46
Premier, Russian, 89
President, U.S., 9, 41, 67, 89, 90*
Press (media), 78, 92, 105
Prime Minister, British, 89
Prisoners, German, 83, 87
Prisoners of War, 83, 87, 107
Promotions, 47, 48, 62, 66*
Prophecy, 44, 59, 97
Punitive Expedition into Mexico, 10, 44
Purple Heart, 48
Remarks, 102, 103, 104, 105, 106, 107
Renault Tank, 50-51*
Repayment of loan, 23
Rescue, drowning boys, 56
Revolutionary War, American, 15, 18, 107
Revolver, pearl-handled, 2-3*
Revolvers, 2-3*, 105
Rhine River, 85
Rhine River valley, 85
Riding, 53
Rights of man, 107
Rocky Mountain Fur Company, 19
Rommel, Erwin, 92
Roosevelt, Franklin D., 67, 89
Rubio, Chihuahua, Mexico, 41, 42
Ruins, Indian (Mexico), 46
Rule the world, 81
Russia, U.S. policy toward, 107
Russian forces, 87
Russian leader, 89
Russian menace, 103
Russian Premier, 89
Russian-occupied territory, 106
Russian torture, 106
Russians, 87, 88, 89, 91, 103, 106, 107
Russians, distrust of, 91
Saber, cavalry, 33
"Saber George" (George Smith Patton, Jr.), 34
Sabers, 33, 34, 40
Sahara Desert, 63
Sailing sloop, 56
Sailing, 27, 56, 97
Saint Mihiel, Battle of, 48

Salem Harbor, Massachusetts, 56
San Gabriel, California, 18
San Miguelito (ranch in Mexico), 41
Savagery, 104
Schooner, 56, 97
Scientific American, 46
Scotland, 15
Sears Roebuck, 62
Second Armored Division, 62, 63
Second Lieutenant of cavalry, 29
Securing testimony, 106
Sense of humor, 45, 46
Seventh Army, 68, 72, 81
Shenandoah Valley (Virginia), 13
Shell shock, 79
Sherman Tank, 82*
Sicily, 67, 68, 72, 81
Sicily, invasion of, 67, 68
Siegfried line, 87
Sierra Blanca, Texas, 40
Sierra Leone, Africa, 65
Signer of the Magna Charta, 15
Sister, 16-17*
"Sixteenth (16th) century man" (George Smith Patton, Jr.), 94
Slapping incident, 70, 71, 72, 73, 75, 102
Slave labor, 107
Slavery, 107
Smith, George H. (step grandfather), 18
Smith, Ophelia (aunt), 30
Son-in-law, 85
Spirit of Camaraderie, 63
Spreckles, Claus, 22, 23
Stalin, Joseph, 89
Step grandfather (paternal), 18
Stephen Cutter Clark's Classical School for Boys, 26
Stockholm, Sweden, 35, 37
Stone-age money, 46
Stuart, J. E. B., 14
Suicide (Julio Cardenas), 42
Sultan of Morocco, 65
Surgeon-General of the American forces, 18
Surrender, German, 91
Swimming, 37
Sympathy, 96, 105
Tank corps, 47, 49, 55
Tank operations, 48
Tank, Renault, 50-51*
Tank warfare, 47, 48, 49, 54, 60, 82
Tanks, 47, 48, 49, 50-51*, 53, 54, 55, 60, 62, 63, 82*, 85, 103
Tanks, first large scale use, 47
Tanks, role in war, 53
Teheran Conference, 89
Teheran, Iran, 89
Temper, 58, 70, 71, 75
Ten-point code for wives, 97
Terrorists, 9
Testimony, securing, 106
Theory of education, 24
Third Army, 83, 85, 87
Third Cavalry, 60
Thirty-eight (.38) caliber revolver, 37
Three-star major general, 66
Three-Hundred Fourth (304th) Brigade, 52
Torture, Russian, 106

111

Totten, Ruth Ellen Patten (daughter), 13
Track, 27, 37
Track, West Point, 27, 37
Trading post, 19
Traffic Accident, 92
Trier, Germany, 85
Trucks, 10
Truman, Harry S., 90*
Tunis, Tunisia, 66
Twenty-second Virginia Regiment, 13
Twenty-two (.22) caliber revolver, 37
U-boats, 64, 65
Uncles & Aunts, 18, 30
Unconditional surrender, German, 91
Understanding, 96, 105
United States citizens, 40
United States Congress, 79, 92
United States policy toward Russia, 107
United States President, 9, 41, 67, 89, 90*
United States Tank Corps, 49
United States Treasury Department (Life Saving Medal of Honor), 56
Universal military training, 104
Valley of the Rhine River, 85
Van Fleet, James A., 84*
Vichy, France, 67
Vichy government (France), 67
Vicksburg, Mississippi, 19
Villa, Francisco "Pancho", 7, 9, 10, 44, 40, 41
Virginia Military Institute, 26, 58
Virginia Regiment, twenty-second, 13
Wallace, Brenton, 71
War against Japan, 88, 91
War alarms, 9
War Department, 54, 76
War, glorification of, 14
War, individuals in, 105
War in North America, fear, 9
War in the Pacific, 88, 91
War, prisoners of, 83, 87, 107
Warfare, 9, 10, 11, 42, 44, 48, 49, 54, 60, 82
Warfare, armored, 48, 49

Warfare, first mechanized, 10, 11, 42, 44
Warfare, guerrilla, 9, 10
Warfare, mechanized, 10, 11, 42, 44, 60
Warfare, tank, 48, 49, 54, 60, 82
Washington, D.C., 59, 92
Washington, George, 15, 18
Washington, John, 15
Washington politicians, 92
Water, ration, 63
Weapons, 2-3*, 34, 105
Weapons (pearl-handled revolver), 2-3*
Wedding, 31
West Point graduation, 29
West Point Military Academy, 26, 27, 29, 31, 37, 58, 95
West Point track, 27, 37
Western Europe, 62
Western world, 89
"When & If" (schooner), 97
Wife, 30, 31, 32, 40, 44, 56, 58, 59, 78, 95, 97
Wife, help or detriment, 31, 32
Wife, influence of, 32
Willie (dog), 86*, 93*
Wilson, Benjamin Davis (grandfather), 19, 20, 21, 22
Wilson, Margaret S. Hereford (grandmother), 21
Wilson, Ruth Smith (mother), 16-17*, 21
Wilson, Woodrow, 9, 41
Wine, 20
Wives, Ten point code for, 97
World War I, 47, 49, 53, 54, 92
World War II, 13, 15, 19, 60, 62, 64, 65, 66*, 67, 68, 69*, 70, 71, 72, 73, 74, 75, 76, 77, 78, 79, 80, 81, 83, 84*, 85, 86*, 87, 88, 89, 90*, 91, 92
Wounded soldiers, 70, 72, 73
Wounds, 48
Wrath, ecstasy of, 104
Writing, 59, 92
Writing (Beatrice), 59
Yacht, 56, 57, 97

ACKNOWLEDGMENTS

Wesley Klug, cover illustration, 42
Third Cavalry Museum, Fort Bliss, Texas, 32
Patton Museum of Cavalry and Armor, cover portrait, title pages, 8, 16-17, 21, 25, 28, 37, 38-39, 50-51, 57, 61, 66, 69, 82, 84, 86, 93, 101
Eisenhower Museum, Abilene, Kansas, 90.
The author wishes to extend special thanks to David A. Holt, Librarian of the Patton Museum of Cavalry and Armor for research and to the museum for supplying most of the illustrations.